AMINATA COOTE

The Battle Is Not Yours

21 Devotions for Spiritual Warfare

First published by Hopelight Publishers 2024

Copyright © 2024 by Aminata Coote

All rights reserved. No part of this publication may be reproduced, stored or transmitted in any form or by any means, electronic, mechanical, photocopying, recording, scanning, or otherwise without written permission from the publisher. It is illegal to copy this book, post it to a website, or distribute it by any other means without permission.

Aminata Coote has no responsibility for the persistence or accuracy of URLs for external or third-party Internet Websites referred to in this publication and does not guarantee that any content on such Websites is, or will remain, accurate or appropriate.

Unless otherwise stated, Scripture quotations are from the ESV Bible.

The Holy Bible, English Standard Version. ESV® Text Edition: 2016. Copyright © 2001 by Crossway Bibles, a publishing ministry of Good News Publishers.

Holy Bible, New Living Translation, copyright © 1996, 2004, 2015 by Tyndale House Foundation. Used by permission of Tyndale House Publishers, Inc., Carol Stream, Illinois 60188. All rights reserved.

Scriptures notated as KJV are from the King James Version of the Bible which is in the public domain.

Holy Bible, New International Version®, NIV® Copyright ©1973, 1978, 1984, 2011 by Biblica, Inc.® Used by permission. All rights reserved worldwide.

Scripture taken from the New King James Version®. Copyright © 1982 by Thomas Nelson. Used by permission. All rights reserved.

First edition

ISBN: 978 976 8334 16 9

This book was professionally typeset on Reedsy.
Find out more at reedsy.com

Contents

Introduction

Hi Friend,

The Bible talks a lot about spiritual warfare, and even though it's something we're aware of as Christians, too often we don't pay close enough attention.

We forget that the "enemy" we see with our physical eyes is not the true enemy.

This devotional is a reminder of who we're fighting and what we're up against. But it's also a reminder of the powerful tools and resources we have at our disposal.

It's a reminder that when we give our battles to the Lord, we'll have victory in and through Him.

This devotional has five sections:

1. Know Your Enemy
2. Gather Your Resources
3. Use Your Weapons
4. Fight the Enemy
5. Victory in Christ

My prayer is that as you go through each section, you'll become better equipped to fight the enemy. I pray that you'll pick up your weapons and claim your victory in Christ Jesus.

What are you waiting for, girlfriend? Let's go to battle.

I

Know Your Enemy

Many times, as believers, we underestimate the power of the enemy. Either that or we don't identify when he's at play in our lives.

1

He's Not Human

For we do not wrestle against flesh and blood, but against the rulers, against the authorities, against the cosmic powers over this present darkness, against the spiritual forces of evil in the heavenly places. – Ephesians 6:12

Have you ever argued with someone without a valid reason? The argument may be about something major or something insignificant, it doesn't matter.

Maybe the person you argued with was a family member, coworker, or friend. Maybe the person was a stranger.

In either case, you walked away from the conversation angry and frustrated. Your entire day had been upended and all the plans you had.

Maybe you spend a few minutes (or hours) stewing about the situation. How dare that person talk to you that way? How could they not understand your vision? Why can't they support you?

At some point, logic may set in and you wonder, why was I even arguing about that in the first place?

If any of these sound, or feel familiar, you may have been

involved in a spiritual battle.

The Oxford Online Dictionary defines battle as a sustained fight between large organized armed forces.

You may disagree with this definition because you're thinking, I'm a Christian. I'm not part of an organized armed force.

Aren't you?

Then why do we have songs like *I'm in the Lord's Army* and *Onward Christian Soldier*? Why does the Bible encourage us to commune with other believers?

Why does Exodus 15:3 call God a "man of war"?

Are you beginning to see it now? Whether we choose to admit it, when we became Christians, we were inducted into the army of God.

One of God's names is Jehovah Sabaoth, which can be translated as The Lord of Armies.

The Collins Online Dictionary defines spiritual[1] as relating to people's thoughts and beliefs, rather than to their bodies and physical surroundings.

Let's put these two definitions together to make our own.

Spiritual warfare is a battle between the Lord's armies and the devil's. This battle relates to our thoughts and beliefs, rather than our bodies and physical surroundings.

This is the reason today's key text is so important. The battle we're fighting is not against a physical person. It's against a spiritual force.

The devil isn't human, so why do we waste our energy and effort fighting him as if he is? Let's not underestimate him or pretend we can fight him in our strength and on our terms.

My friend, the enemy will use the people around us to engage

---

[1]   https://www.collinsdictionary.com/dictionary/english/spiritual

us in spiritual warfare.

He'll tangle us up in petty disputes and disagreements because he knows it will distract us from our purpose.

When you are engaging in a physical battle, breathe. Remind yourself that the enemy is not physical. He's not human. He's a spiritual being and we can't defeat him with physical weapons.

We'll talk about our weapons later, but for today, just breathe.

Prayer

Dear Heavenly Father,

Thank You for the reminder that I'm engaged in a spiritual battle against an enemy that's not human. Help me identify his tactics and discern when he's using the people around me to distract, disturb, or destroy.

Open my spiritual eyes to see the hosts of Your armies that surround me. Thank You for helping me through this battle. In Jesus' name, Amen.

2

A Roaring Lion

Be sober-minded; be watchful. Your adversary the devil prowls around like a roaring lion, seeking someone to devour. 1 Peter 5:8

I f you're anything like me, the idea of a prowling lion has you quaking in your boots. Or at least, making a mental note to stay away from places where lions would be free to roam around.

The fact that Peter compares the devil to a roaring lion intrigues me. Let me explain. Jesus is called the Lion of the tribe of Judah (Revelation 5:5) and the image we get is one of power and might.

Yet, the opposite is true when we think of a prowling lion. A prowling lion evokes fear and anxiety. The idea of the devil being a roaring lion on the prowl is scary.

Could it be because our impression of a roaring lion is that he's about to attack? I found a fascinating article about why lions roar[2]. I encourage you to read it, but we'll focus on the reasons our enemy, the devil, would "roar" at us.

1. Lions roar to show dominance. Lions are called the king of the jungle because of their power and strength. They don't fear any other animals because of this superiority. A single roar would be enough to remind the other animals of their place in the food chain.

2. Lions roar to express power. Did you know a lion's roar can be heard up to five miles away? Can you imagine how terrifying it must be for a sheep to hear that roar and know that a predator is in the vicinity?

If I were a sheep, I'd be running toward my Master. I wouldn't deviate to the right or the left. I would run as fast as my little legs could scurry and not stop until I was trembling in the arms of my Shepherd.

3. Lions roar to mark territory. Every animal has a way to claim what they consider theirs. Dogs urinate over their stuff. Cats rub themselves over things they claim. Lions roar.

I'm pretty sure if one of the lesser animals, like say a zebra, had laid claim to a patch of land, they'd scurry away as soon as they heard that horrific roar.

4. Lions roar to coordinate an attack. Okay, one lion is bad. A pride of lions? Terrifying.

---

[2] Discover the 10 Reasons Why Lions Roar https://a-z-animals.com/blog/disc over-the-reasons-why-lions-roar/

Can you see how the enemy has used any of the tactics above against us? Have you seen how he's successfully used his roar against us?

Do you know the other significant thing about this imagery of the roaring lion? The Bible calls us sheep and goats. Do you know what lions do to sheep and goats? They eat them.

Gulp!

I believe the Holy Spirit inspired Peter to write this imagery as a reminder that the enemy is more powerful than we give him credit for.

As sheep, we need to stay close to the Great Shepherd. Jesus can battle the lion on our behalf because He is the Great Lion.

The devil is a lion, Christ is *the* Lion. Jesus will always defeat the enemy, which is why we should leave the battle to Him.

Prayer

Father,

Thank You for the Good Shepherd. You knew we'd need protection against the evil one and so you sent us Your Son—the Great Lion who'd fight for us against the roaring lion.

Help us return to the fold of our Master and seek shelter and protection with our Shepherd. In Jesus' name, we pray, Amen.

3

The Great Deceiver

*Now war arose in heaven, Michael and his angels fighting against
the dragon. And the dragon and his angels fought back,
but he was defeated, and there was no longer any place for them in
heaven.
And the great dragon was thrown down, that ancient serpent, who
is called the devil and Satan, the deceiver of the whole world—he
was thrown down to the earth, and his angels were thrown down
with him. Revelation 12:7-9*

Revelation 12:7 begins with words that seem inconceivable to us, "Now war arose in heaven".

When we think about heaven, we imagine a peaceful place where God lives. We picture roads paved with gold and the celestial beings worshiping the Creator.

We envision safety, peace, and love. Not war or epic battles. Not angels choosing the wrong side or being cast out of heaven.

Yet, that's exactly what happened. Satan deceived one-third of the angels and God and threw them to the earth with the devil.

The Oxford Online Dictionary defines deceive in the following ways:

1. Give (someone) a mistaken impression.
2. Fail to admit to oneself that something is true.

Hmm, that's interesting. But let's dig a little deeper.

The word translated as deceived in Revelation 12:9 is the Greek planáō[3], (pronounced plan-ah'-o). Planáō could also have been translated as to (cause to) roam (from safety, truth, or virtue). It could have been translated to mean go astray, deceive, err, seduce, or wander.

Isn't that a fitting depiction of what the enemy does?

He gives people a mistaken impression about something he refuses to admit is true and then he seduces them away from safety.

My friend, the Bible calls the devil the Great Deceiver, which means he's excellent at what he does.

Sometimes, we forget this about the enemy. We forget that he's the father of lies (John 8:44) and that his entire plan is to deceive humanity (Revelation 12:9, 12).

The devil plans to kill, steal, and destroy (John 10:10). Be on your guard.

I don't say this to make you afraid. No. It's a reminder not to underestimate the enemy. A reminder that there is One we can depend on.

Jesus came so that we might have abundant life (John 10:10) and victory over the evil one (Luke 10:19).

Draw close to Jesus and allow your Savior to protect you from

---

[3] "G4105 - planaō - Strong's Greek Lexicon (KJV)." Blue Letter Bible. Web. 7 Jan, 2024. .

the enemy.

Prayer

Dear Heavenly Father,

Help me not to underestimate the devil. He deceived a third of the angels in heaven. Help me be on my guard so as not to get drawn in by his deceptions.

Thank You for sending Your Son Jesus, who can defeat the enemy.

Thank You for the plan of salvation that makes it possible for me to have eternal life and to one day spend time with You in heaven. In Your name, I pray, Amen.

4

Angel of Light

And no wonder, for even Satan disguises himself as an angel of light. 2 Corinthians 11:14

Paul's second letter to the church at Corinth took an interesting turn in chapter 11.

While Paul appreciated the church's hospitality, he feared it had opened them up to false doctrines because they welcomed everyone.

The Corinthians didn't apply discernment to those who came to teach doctrine—even when it contradicted what Paul had taught them about Christ.

This put them in a precarious position. False prophets—people who had presented themselves as followers of Christ when they weren't—had deceived them.

Paul accused these false prophets of disguising themselves and compared them to the devil, who masquerades as an angel of light (2 Corinthians 11:13-14).

There's so much to unpack here, so let's take it in stages.

According to the Oxford Online Dictionary, a disguise is a

means of altering one's appearance to conceal one's identity.

The false prophets had deliberately misled the church of Corinth about who they were, just as Satan adopts the guise of an angel of light to mislead us.

When we think about angels, we picture messengers of God. Celestial beings who stand in the presence of Jehovah and do His will.

We forget that the devil and his minions are *fallen* angels.

We've bought into the deception that the devil will come at us looking like the images we've created to express who he is.

He could appear to us that way, but he may not.

Don't expect the enemy to come wearing leathery red skin and horns. He's called the son of the morning and masks himself as an angel of light.

The lesson for the Corinthians and us is the same: not everything or everyone that looks good is.

Not every "angel" is a messenger of God.

We can only see through their disguises when we know who God is and can recognize His voice.

My friend, God desires to be known by you and will reveal Himself to you in countless ways. The only way the enemy won't deceive you is if you have a personal relationship with God.

Prayer

Dear Heavenly Father,

I don't want to be deceived by the enemy. Help me spend time in Your Word and to build a relationship with You so that I can recognize Your voice.

Protect me from the evil one and grant me discernment to recognize those who are disguising themselves as Your messengers.

Thank You for hearing and answering my prayers. In Jesus' name, Amen.

II

Gather Your Resources

*Now that we know our enemy, let's identify our
weapons and gather our resources.*

5

Divine Power and Authority

For though we walk in the flesh, we are not waging war according to the flesh. For the weapons of our warfare are not of the flesh but have divine power to destroy strongholds. 2 Corinthians 10:3-4

After reading about all the power the devil has, maybe you're wondering how you can go against this powerful enemy. Don't worry. God has given us every weapon we will need to defeat him.

The first thing we need to understand about these weapons is that they're neither physical nor human.

This makes perfect sense. We're not battling against humans or creatures of the flesh, so we need weapons that can defeat the beings we're fighting.

But what kinds of weapons do we have?

Paul says they have "divine power" and can "destroy strongholds".

Wait, what?

Let's dig a little deeper.

The word translated as divine is the Greek word theós[4], (pronounced theh'-os) and is used in the Bible to refer to the things of God, including His counsels, interests, or things due to Him.

The word translated as stronghold is the Greek word ochýrōma[5], (pronounced okh-oo'-ro-mah). Ochýrōma is used in the Bible to represent a castle, stronghold, or fortress.

The Oxford Online Dictionary defines stronghold in two ways:

1. A place that has been fortified so as to protect it against attack.
2. A place where a particular cause or belief is strongly defended or upheld.

I'd like to combine all the definitions. Remember, we're in a war. Imagine that the enemy is in a fortified castle. Our weapons are powerful enough to bring down those walls.

In Luke 10, we see this in action. Jesus called seventy of His disciples and sent them out into every city (Luke 10:1).

Before He sent the disciples, Jesus encouraged them and gave them some instructions. They obeyed Him and returned exultant because of the miracles they'd performed.

In response, Jesus said:

> *Behold, I have given you authority to tread on serpents*
> *and scorpions, and over all the power of the enemy, and*

---

4 "G2316 - theos - Strong's Greek Lexicon (KJV)." Blue Letter Bible. Web. 7 Jan, 2024. .

5 "G3794 - ochyrōma - Strong's Greek Lexicon (KJV)." Blue Letter Bible. Web. 7 Jan, 2024. .

nothing shall hurt you (Luke 10:19).

The devil isn't a flesh and blood enemy, but God has given us mighty weapons, including power and authority over him. When we wield our weapons in Jesus' name, we'll have victory.

Prayer

Dear Lord,

Thank You for these mighty weapons You've given me against the enemy. When I'm in a spiritual battle, remind me that my weapons are not carnal, but divinely powerful.

Help me exercise the power and authority You've given me to tear down any strongholds in my life or my family.

In Jesus' mighty name, I pray, Amen.

6

A Two-edged Sword

For the word of God is living and active, sharper than any two-edged sword, piercing to the division of soul and of spirit, of joints and of marrow, and discerning the thoughts and intentions of the heart. Hebrews 4:12

One of the more powerful weapons we have in this spiritual battle is the Word of God. The Bible is the story of God's people. It shows us the faithfulness of God despite the fickleness of humanity. It teaches us the nature and character of God.

The Bible shows us what God expects from His people and how to live up to His expectations.

Here are some things the Bible says about itself:

This Book of the Law shall not depart from your mouth, but you shall meditate on it day and night, so that you may be careful to do according to all that is written in it. For then you will make your way prosperous, and then you will have good success (Joshua 1:8).

The law of the Lord is perfect, reviving the soul; the testimony of the Lord is sure, making wise the simple;

the precepts of the Lord are right, rejoicing the heart; the commandment of the Lord is pure, enlightening the eyes;

the fear of the Lord is clean, enduring forever; the rules of the Lord are true, and righteous altogether.

More to be desired are they than gold, even much fine gold; sweeter also than honey and drippings of the honeycomb.

Moreover, by them is your servant warned; in keeping them there is great reward (Psalm 19:7-11).

So shall my word be that goes out from my mouth; it shall not return to me empty, but it shall accomplish that which I purpose, and shall succeed in the thing for which I sent it (Isaiah 55:11).

All Scripture is breathed out by God and profitable for teaching, for reproof, for correction, and for training in righteousness

that the man of God may be complete, equipped for every good work (2 Timothy 3:16-17).

For whatever was written in former days was written for our instruction, that through endurance and through the encouragement of the Scriptures we might have hope (Romans 15:4).

There are many other verses, but the point is this: the Word of God is powerful. Use it!

The author of Hebrews compares the Word of God to a double-edged sword. I'd like you to visualize someone using a sword[6] in combat. It would take great skill to use that weapon and not hurt yourself.

Because here's the thing about God's Word: it's powerful enough to expose the flaws, failings, and weaknesses of our enemy...and our own. No one is exempt from the shining light of God's truth.

As the author of Hebrews explains,

> *Nothing in all creation is hidden from God. Everything is naked and exposed before his eyes, and he is the one to whom we are accountable (Hebrews 4:13 NLT).*

Study the Word of God. Allow it to transform you into the likeness of Christ. And then, only then, should you attempt to wield it in battle.

Prayer

Lord,

Thank You for the two-edged sword and for caring about me enough to want me to be changed.

Please create in me a desire to read and study Your Word. Help me become so hungry for Your Word that I will make the time to develop a Bible study habit.

---

[6] Learn more about the two-edged sword at https://swordis.com/blog/what-is-a-double-edged-sword/

Equip me to use Your Word wisely. In Jesus' name, I pray, Amen.

7

The Power of Prayer

Let us then with confidence draw near to the throne of grace, that
we may receive mercy and find grace to help in time of need.
Hebrews 4:16

Some Christians are uncertain about prayer. Should they pray to God the Father, Jesus Christ, or the Holy Spirit? Are there some things they shouldn't pray about? Should they only go to God about the "big" things?

Are they bothering Him when they pray about the "small" stuff? Who decides what's "small stuff" and what isn't?

Can prayer be too much or too little? How do you know when it's time to praise, especially if God hasn't answered your prayer?

How do you know if God's answer is yes, no, or maybe?

This book is too short to provide you with the answers to those questions, except to recommend that you study the prayers in the Bible.

As you study the prayers, spend time in communion with God and ask Him your questions. He'll answer you.

I love the way the King James Version renders today's verse:

> *Let us therefore* **come boldly** *unto the throne of grace,*
> *that we may obtain mercy, and find grace to help in time*
> *of need — Hebrews 4:16 KJV (emphasis mine).*

The word translated as boldly is the Greek parrhēsía[7], (pronounced par-rhay-see'-ah).

Parrhēsía could also have been translated as out-spokenness, frankness, bluntness, assurance, confidence, freely, openly, or plainly.

Parrhēsía is used in the Bible when referring to:

- freedom in speaking, unreservedness in speech
- (speaking) openly, frankly, i.e. without concealment
- (speaking) without ambiguity or circumlocution
- (speaking) without the use of figures and comparisons
- free and fearless confidence, cheerful courage, boldness, or assurance.

So what does parrhēsía mean for us?

It means that we can go before God without hesitation. We don't have to worry about whether we have the right words. We don't have to worry that we're "bothering" God.

Jehovah is our Father. He invites us to come before Him whenever we have a need. He invites us to lay our hearts bare before Him.

A word of warning: sincerity is important to God. Do not think

---

7 "G3954 - parrēsia - Strong's Greek Lexicon (KJV)." Blue Letter Bible. Web. 7 Jan, 2024. .

you can manipulate or bargain with Him. That's not the type of relationship He desires with us.

In God's throne room, we'll find grace, mercy, and help in our time of need.

Prayer is a weapon. But it's only effective if we learn how to use it.

Prayer

Abba Father,

I don't always know what to say or how to pray. Thank You for the Holy Spirit, who intercedes on my behalf.

Thank You for caring about me enough to want to help me. For caring enough to invite me into Your inner sanctum.

Remind me, Lord, that prayer is a weapon—one that You've gifted me with and that is powerful against the evil one.

Guide my prayer life, Lord. Teach me how to pray, and how to come boldly into Your throne room. In Jesus' name, I pray, Amen.

8

The Armor of God

Therefore take up the whole armor of God, that you may be able to withstand in the evil day, and having done all, to stand firm.
Ephesians 6:13

One of the most crucial pieces of equipment in warfare is the armor. If you have nothing to hide behind or to shield you from the enemy, your ability to strike is severely limited.

The apostle Paul encourages believers to take up the "whole armor of God". That suggests to me that there are several pieces to the armor (more on that later).

The word translated as take up is the Greek analambánō[8], (pronounced an-al-am-ban'-o).

Analambánō is used in the Bible to mean raise or to take up (a thing in order to carry or use it).

Because you can take something up for many reasons: to

---

8 "G353 - analambanō - Strong's Greek Lexicon (KJV)." Blue Letter Bible. Web. 7 Jan, 2024. .

give it away, to toss it, to safeguard it. This word choice was deliberate.

The word translated as armor is the Greek panoplía[9], (pronounced pan-op-lee'-ah).

Panoplía is used in the Bible when referring to complete armor, including shield, sword, lance, helmet, greaves[10], and breastplate.

The apostle goes into detail about each piece of armor and how to use it. Have you taken up the armor of God? Are you using it?

Let's imagine for a moment a modern soldier going into battle. His unit gave him an army tanker and assigned him to the front line of the war.

He goes to the battlefield on foot because he considers the tanker an optional piece of equipment.

When he gets to the front line, there's a line of armored tanks squared off against him and his fellow soldiers.

How do you think this lone soldier will fare in the battle?

God has given us a suit of armor to use in spiritual warfare. What are you going to do with it?

If we don't take up the armor of God, *intending to use it*, it will be ineffective.

What are you waiting for? Take up your armor, my friend.

---

[9] "G3833 - panoplia - Strong's Greek Lexicon (KJV)." Blue Letter Bible. Web. 7 Jan, 2024. .

[10] Greaves are a piece of defensive armor which reached from the foot to the knee and thus protected the shin of the wearer. It was made of leather or brass.

 Orr, James, M.A., D.D. General Editor. "Entry for 'GREAVES'". "International Standard Bible Encyclopedia". 1915. https://www.biblestudytools.com/dictionary/greaves/

Prayer

Dear Lord,

Thank You for equipping me with a shield of armor. Give me the strength to take up this armor and to use every resource in this battle against the enemy.

In Jesus' name, I pray. Amen.

III

Use Your Weapons

God has given us powerful resources to use against our enemy. It's time for us to learn to use them.

9

Put On Your Armor

Finally, be strong in the Lord and in the strength of his might. Put on the whole armor of God, that you may be able to stand against the schemes of the devil. Ephesians 6:10-11

So you've taken up the armor of God and intend to use it. The first step is to put on your gear.

When you read Ephesians 6:14-18, you'll realize that there are several pieces to your armor and that each has a purpose. It makes no sense to get partially dressed.

The reason we put on our armor, according to Paul, is to protect ourselves against the schemes of the enemy.

The word translated as schemes is the Greek methodeía[11], (pronounced meth-od-i'-ah).

Methodeía could also have been translated to mean travesty, trickery, or wile. It is used in the Bible when referring to cunning arts, deceit, craft, or trickery.

---

[11] "G3180 - methodeia - Strong's Greek Lexicon (KJV)." Blue Letter Bible. Web. 7 Jan, 2024. .

This makes sense when we remember the enemy sometimes wears a disguise. The Bible has described the devil as:

- A roaring lion (1 Peter 5:8).
- An angel of light (2 Corinthians 11:14).
- The father of lies and a murderer (John 8:44).
- A great dragon (Revelation 12:9).
- An ancient serpent (Revelation 20:2).

These are but some things the Bible says about the devil. Is it any wonder that we need protection from him?

But God has given us armor that protects us. This armor is only effective if we take it up and put it on.

When we put on the armor of God, we can resist the devil. Wearing the armor of God isn't an invitation to complacency.

It's never a case that you'll put it on once and that's it. Just as you get dressed every day, the armor is to be put on daily.

But what does it mean to put on the armor of God?

Wearing the armor of God means regular Bible reading and study. It means time spent in prayer. Wearing the armor means asking for forgiveness when we sin and covering ourselves in the righteousness of Christ.

When we are circumspect about what we consume—not just the food we eat. But also what we listen to and watch. The books we read and our conversations all reinforce or weaken the armor.

We can't fail to cultivate good habits while continuing with negative ones and expect to come out of the battle unscathed.

God gave us His armor because He wants us to use it. Don't disregard this vital weapon.

Prayer

Dear Heavenly Father,

Thank You for Your armor that will help me withstand the attacks of the enemy. Remind me I need to put Your armor on every day.

If there's a piece of armor that I'm not using effectively, please reveal it to me and show me how to utilize it for maximum impact.

In Your name, I pray. Amen.

10

Refute Every Tongue

"No weapon that is fashioned against you shall succeed, and you shall refute every tongue that rises against you in judgment. This is the heritage of the servants of the Lord and their vindication from me, declares the Lord." Isaiah 54:17

Words are powerful. This is something we all know, but somehow don't put enough emphasis on.

I find it interesting that Isaiah told the Israelites no weapon formed against them would prosper. And then, in the next breath, the prophet encouraged them to "refute every tongue that rises against" them.

The word translated as refute is the Hebrew râsha‘[12], (pronounced raw-shah'). Râsha‘ could also have been translated as condemn.

Let's talk about the power of the tongue for a second. Proverbs 18:21 tells us that death and life are in the power of the tongue.

---

[12] "H7561 - rāšaʿ - Strong's Hebrew Lexicon (KJV)." Blue Letter Bible. Web. 7 Jan, 2024. .

The New Living Translation renders it this way:

> *The tongue can bring death or life; those who love to talk
> will reap the consequences.*

Wow. Let that sink in for a second.

The words we speak can produce life. Our words can also produce death.

If you think about your life for a moment, you may identify times and areas where you experienced either life or death because of someone's words.

Maybe you had a teacher or someone in authority speak positive things over your life and you saw it come to fruition. Or maybe a dream of yours experienced a premature death because of something that was said to you.

If we go back to the Garden of Eden, words are the weapon the enemy used to defeat Eve. It's the weapon he's successfully wielded throughout the ages and is the one he relies on now.

But we can defeat the enemy because our words have power, too. The power that comes from God.

Jehovah is the Creator of words. Through His Words, He created all things, including us. He's given us this creative power to use our words to create or to destroy. Use your power wisely.

Instead of listening to words that speak death over your circumstances, speak life.

Instead of speaking death over yourself and your loved ones, speak life.

Speaking may be as simple as words of affirmation. I encourage you to search the Scriptures for verses and use them as a starting point for your affirmations.

Rebuke any tongue—including your own—that speaks defeat

over your life and what you can accomplish.

Prayer

Dear Heavenly Father,

Thank You for this reminder that words are powerful. Help me refute any words that are spoken against me, including those that I say to myself.

Speaking positive words is not always easy, but I submit my tongue to You and ask You to keep it under control.

Thank You for the power and authority to speak words of life and healing. In Jesus' name, Amen.

11

Truth Sets Us Free

So Jesus said to the Jews who had believed him, "If you abide in my word, you are truly my disciples, and you will know the truth, and the truth will set you free." John 8:31-32

Today, the definition of truth depends on whom you ask. This makes deciding what is true difficult.

The Oxford Online Dictionary defines true in the following ways:

- in accordance with fact or reality
- real or actual
- accurate or exact
- accurately conforming to (a standard or expectation); faithful to
- honest (archaic definition).

The one thing all these definitions have in common is accuracy. Jesus told His disciples, "If you abide in my word...you will know the truth", so let's dig a little deeper.

The word translated as abide is the Greek ménō[13], (pronounced men'-o). Ménō could also have been translated as dwell, endure, be present, remain, stand, or tarry.

Each of these words indicates a settling in or time spent somewhere.

The word translated as truth is the Greek alétheia[14], (pronounced al-ay'-thi-a).

Alétheia is used in the Bible when referring to:

- what is true in any matter under consideration
- what is true in things appertaining to God and the duties of man, moral and religious truth
- truth as a personal excellence, among other things.

The word translated as free is the Greek eleutheróō[15], (pronounced el-yoo-ther-o'-o).

Eleutheróō could also be translated to mean: to liberate, to exempt (from moral, ceremonial, or mortal liability), deliver, or make free.

Eleutheróō is used in the Bible to mean set at liberty: from the dominion of sin.

I know those were a lot of definitions, but this is where it gets better. If we were to paraphrase John 8:31-32, it would look something like this:

---

[13] "G3306 - menō - Strong's Greek Lexicon (KJV)." Blue Letter Bible. Web. 7 Jan, 2024. .

[14] "G225 - alētheia - Strong's Greek Lexicon (KJV)." Blue Letter Bible. Web. 7 Jan, 2024. .

[15] "G1659 - eleutheroō - Strong's Greek Lexicon (KJV)." Blue Letter Bible. Web. 7 Jan, 2024. .

*If you spend time in my word, you are truly my disciples,
and you will know the things that are true pertaining to
God. This truth will liberate you from sin.*

As we engage in spiritual warfare, the ability to discern truth is critical. Remember, the enemy is a liar and a thief. He disguises himself as things he's not. If we can't determine what's true, we've already lost the battle.

Truth is found in Christ. Jesus *is* Truth. When we wield the Word of God, we gain victory over the enemy's lies.

Prayer

Dear Lord,

The Bible tells us that Jesus is the way, the truth, and the life. It tells us You are light and in You, there's no darkness at all. Since I'm made in Your image and have accepted Jesus as Lord and Savior, it means that light and truth dwell in me.

Help me abide in Your Word, to crave spending time with You, so I can say, like David, that I've hidden Your Word in my heart.

I want to be free from sin, Lord, so I choose You. Sanctify me by Your Word, Lord, in Jesus' name. Amen.

12

Capture Every Thought

We destroy arguments and every lofty opinion raised against the knowledge of God, and take every thought captive to obey Christ, 2 Corinthians 10:5

L et us revisit the temptation of Eve in the Garden of Eden in Genesis 3. The temptation began with a seemingly innocuous question:

> *"Did God really say you must not eat the fruit from any of the trees in the garden?" (Genesis 3:1 NLT)*

Eve quickly responds in defense of God with all the fruits she's able to eat and the one she cannot.

Eve is adamant that if she even touches the fruit from the Tree of the Knowledge of Good and Evil, she'll die.

> *"You won't die!" the serpent replied to the woman. "God knows that your eyes will be opened as soon as you eat it, and you will be like God, knowing both good and evil."*

(Genesis 3:4–5 NLT)

We don't know what happened in the moments between the devil's statements and Eve's actions, but I believe Eve had thoughts.

They may have been similar to these.

Why doesn't God want us to eat from this tree?

I want to be more like God. Doesn't He want me to be more like Him?

I won't really die if I eat the fruit, will I?

Why did God tell me I'd die when the serpent says I won't?

You may have noticed a similar pattern in your life. Before you sin, there are thoughts.

James puts it this way:

> *Temptation comes from our own desires, which entice us and drag us away.*
>
> *These desires give birth to sinful actions. And when sin is allowed to grow, it gives birth to death. (James 1:14–15 NLT)*

The way to subjugate our temptation to sin is to "take captive every thought to make it obedient to Christ" (2 Corinthians 10:5 NIV).

Okay, I get it. You have a gazillion thoughts a day. How are you supposed to "capture" every one of them?

You probably won't. But what you may not realize is that a lot of your thoughts are on repeat.

Think about what you're thinking about. Warfare sometimes starts with a thought.

The enemy lies to us and tells us things that sound good but are deceptive. The trouble is that these thoughts sound like us.

The key is to subject your thoughts to the Philippians 4:8 test.

- Is it true?
- Is it honest?
- Is it just?
- Is it pure?
- Is it lovely?
- Is there any virtue in it?
- Is there anything praiseworthy?

If it passes all these tests, only then is that thought allowed to take up residence in your heart and mind.

Examine every thought and compare it against the truth of God's Word.

Prayer

Dear God,

I have a million thoughts a day and it seems impossible to examine each of them to see if they align with Your Word. But what is impossible for me is 100 percent possible with You.

Help me check my thoughts against Your Word to find the truth. Because, Lord, it is the truth that will set me free.

Thank You for hearing and answering my prayer, in Jesus' name. Amen.

IV

Fight the Enemy

You've gathered your intel on the enemy. You've trained with your weapons. It's time to fight.

13

Keep Your Mind on Christ

*You keep him in perfect peace whose mind is stayed on you, because
he trusts in you. Isaiah 26:3*

Sometimes, I wish I could read the Bible in its original
language. Today's verse is one reason for that. In
Hebrew, this verse reads:

```
āṣ
nar šālôm šālôm šālôm ēṣyer āḵsma kî āṭḥba.
```

The word translated as peace is the Hebrew šālôm or shâlôwm[16]
(pronounced shaw-lome).

Shâlôwm could also have been translated to mean safe, well,
happy, friendly, welfare, favour, good health, perfect, peace, or
prosperity.

Shâlôwm is used in the Bible when referring to:

---

[16] "Isaiah 26 (KJV) - Thou wilt keep [him] in." Blue Letter Bible. Web. 7 Jan,
2024. .

- completeness, soundness, welfare, peace
- completeness (in number)
- safety, soundness (in body)
- peace, quiet, tranquillity, contentment
- peace, friendship (of human relationships or with God especially in covenant relationship)
- peace (from war)
- peace (as adjective).

Shâlôwm is also the same word translated as perfect. Isn't that mind-blowing?

When we fix our minds on God, we remember how powerful He is and how powerless the enemy is in comparison.

This complete peace is ours because we have confidence in what God can do. We may not understand *how* He will do it, or know *when* He will act, but we can be sure He will.

How do we fix our minds on Christ?

It begins with the reading and studying of the Bible. As we ingest God's Word, we learn more about who He is. We get exposed to His character and what He expects from us.

We meditate on His Words and think about what we read each day. It will sneak into our conversations as we strive to get a better understanding of what the passage of Scripture means.

We'll talk about the Bible with our children. Our friends and family. On social media. After a while, we'll realize that we crave this time with God.

When we fix our minds on Christ, even though our circumstances may be less than ideal, we'll have peace.

Peace that makes no sense to those not serving God.

Peace that gets us through our daily spiritual battles.

Fixing our minds on Christ gives us peace because, though the enemy may win some skirmishes, the battle belongs to the Lord.

Prayer

Abba Father,

I'm claiming shâlôwm—the peace that surpasses all understanding. The peace that is mine because of who You are.

Father, the battle rages and it is vicious, but I have peace because I trust You. I know that You've already defeated the evil one. All I have to do is trust You, so I will.

Thank You for Your shâlôwm, Lord. May it be a beacon to those who have not yet accepted You, showing them the way to eternal life and victory in the battle. In Jesus' name, Amen.

14

Show No Fear

Have I not commanded you? Be strong and courageous. Do not be frightened, and do not be dismayed, for the Lord your God is with you wherever you go. Joshua 1:9

The book of Joshua begins with a change of guards. In Deuteronomy 34, we read about Moses's death, burial, and how the Israelites mourned for him.

Then we turn the page and God is talking to Joshua about his new commission[17].

God reminded Joshua of the boundaries of the Promised Land and told him no one could stand against him because God was with him.

I'm certain these assurances bolstered Joshua's courage. He would follow in the footsteps of Moses, one of the greatest leaders of his time.

What I find intriguing is the number of times God tells Joshua

---

[17] There was a time gap between Moses's death and God's charge. This phrasing was used as a literary device.

to be brave.

- Be strong and courageous because you will lead these people into the Promised Land (Joshua 1:6).
- Be strong and very courageous so that you can obey all the instructions Moses gave you (Joshua 1:7).
- Be strong and courageous! Don't be afraid or discouraged for I, the LORD your God, is with you wherever you go (Joshua 1:9).

Faith requires courage. It takes courage to obey the Law of God in a world that likes to pretend He doesn't exist.

It takes courage to go after your God-given dreams, especially when you have people telling you all the reasons it's impossible.

It takes courage to face down the enemy because you're aware of how little power you have when you stand against him on your own.

I completely understand. We have oodles of reasons to be afraid. But—

Our job is to show no fear. Our task is to go into battle, though the enemy is more powerful than we are. And here's why.

We have an excellent reason not to be afraid: the Lord is with us.

I feel the need to repeat this: *the Lord is with us*.

The Lord–Jehovah Sabaoth, Lord of Armies, Commander of a host of angels–is with us.

The Lord–omnipotent, omniscient, omnipresent, Creator of everything–is with us.

The Lord–faithful, loving, gracious God–is with us.

God is with us, we shall not fail (Psalm 46:5). Go forth in the battle, my friend, and show no fear.

Prayer

Dear Lord,

Fear sometimes holds me back from doing what needs to be done. Remind me that You are with me and I'm not fighting this battle alone.

As long as I trust in You and are obedient, You will grant me victory over the enemy.

Even so, fear is a human emotion, one I'm not always able to turn off. Please help me be courageous even when I'm not feeling brave.

Your Holy Spirit abides within me, Lord, I will not fail. In Jesus' name, Amen.

15

Fight the Good Fight

Fight the good fight of the faith. Take hold of the eternal life to which you were called and about which you made the good confession in the presence of many witnesses. 1 Timothy 6:12

If anyone can talk about their experience with spiritual warfare, it's the apostle Paul. In his second letter to the church at Corinth, the apostle wrote:

Are they servants of Christ? (I am out of my mind to talk like this.) I am more. I have worked much harder, been in prison more frequently, been flogged more severely, and been exposed to death again and again.

Five times I received from the Jews the forty lashes minus one.

Three times I was beaten with rods, once I was pelted with stones, three times I was shipwrecked, I spent a night and a day in the open sea,

I have been constantly on the move. I have been in danger from rivers, in danger from bandits, in danger from my fellow Jews, in danger from Gentiles; in danger in the city, in danger in the country, in danger at sea; and in danger from false believers.

I have labored and toiled and have often gone without sleep; I have known hunger and thirst and have often gone without food; I have been cold and naked.

Besides everything else, I face daily the pressure of my concern for all the churches.

Who is weak, and I do not feel weak? Who is led into sin, and I do not inwardly burn? (2 Corinthians 11:23-29 NIV)

Paul had been through the wringer and back—and that was before they executed him for being a follower of Christ.

Yet, he could pen these words to Timothy. While advising his honorary son about the issues with the church at Ephesus, Paul took the time to encourage Timothy to remain steadfast in his faith. Paul told Timothy to fight and hold fast.

The word translated as fight is the Greek agōnízomai[18], (pronounced ag-o-nid'-zom-ahee). Agōnízomai literally means to compete for a prize. Figuratively agōnízomai means to contend with an adversary.

The word translated as take hold is the Greek epilambáno-mai[19], (pronounced ep-ee-lam-ban'-om-ahee). Epilambáno-mai could have been translated as seize, catch, or take.

Epilambánomai is used metaphorically in the Bible to mean

---

[18] "G75 - agōnizomai - Strong's Greek Lexicon (KJV)." Blue Letter Bible. Web. 7 Jan, 2024. .

[19] "G1949 - epilambanomai - Strong's Greek Lexicon (KJV)." Blue Letter Bible. Web. 7 Jan, 2024. .

to rescue one from peril, to help, succour.

Hmm.

In other words, we're to fight the good fight of faith as if we're contending with an enemy for a prize.

We're to grab hold of eternal life as if we're rescuing it from peril. Because we are!

This is a battle, sweet friend. And the only way through it is to fight. Fight the good fight of faith that you may stand against the evil one and claim the reward promised by your Heavenly Father.

Prayer

Dear Lord,

Teach me to fight this spiritual battle to win. You've given me powerful resources to use against the enemy. Remind me to use every weapon I have in this battle.

I want to say at the end of my life that I fought a good fight and finished the course You set in front of me.

Thank You for hearing my prayers and aiding me in this battle. In Jesus' name, Amen.

16

Walk in the Spirit

But I say, walk by the Spirit, and you will not gratify the desires of the flesh. Galatians 5:16

There are two forces at war in this spiritual battle: God and the devil. The spirit and the flesh.

The Lord wants us to live in the Spirit, where we receive victory over sin. The devil wants us to give in to every base, fleshy desire.

In his letter to the Galatians, Paul reminded them if they lived according to the guidance of the Holy Spirit, they wouldn't fall prey to the desires of the flesh.

Paul writes:

> *The sinful nature wants to do evil, which is just the opposite of what the Spirit wants. And the Spirit gives us desires that are the opposite of what the sinful nature desires. These two forces are constantly fighting each other, so you are not free to carry out your good intentions. —Galatians 5:17 NLT*

As we strive to gain victory in spiritual warfare, we must master the flesh. The only way to do so is to subjugate our flesh to the will of God.

Before His crucifixion, Jesus told His disciples,

> *And I will ask the Father, and he will give you another advocate to help you and be with you forever— the Spirit of truth. The world cannot accept him, because it neither sees him nor knows him. But you know him, for he lives with you and will be in you.* —John 14:16-17 NIV

The Holy Spirit lives in us.

He gives us power and strength. When we lean on Him, He gives us victory to resist the evil one.

So, how do we get the Holy Spirit to make His home in our hearts?

It begins with an acknowledgment that God is Sovereign in our lives. When we accept Jesus as Lord and Savior, we can invite the Holy Spirit to dwell in us.

As we spend more time in prayer and Bible study, we commune with the Father, the Son, and the Holy Spirit.

We can't fight the enemy on our own. It's the Holy Spirit who fights in us and through us to defeat the evil one.

Prayer

Dear Heavenly Father,

Thank You for the gift of the Holy Spirit. The fleshy part of me wants to do things that go against who You are and what You expect of me.

Please send the Spirit of Truth to dwell within me so that I might not sin against You. In Jesus' name, Amen.

V

Victory in Christ

God has given us every weapon we need to fight the enemy. Our greatest resource is Christ. It is through Jesus, and because of Him, that we will be victorious over the evil one.

17

Submit to God

Submit yourselves therefore to God. Resist the devil, and he will flee from you. James 4:7

People in today's society sometimes treat submission like a dirty word. It creates an impression of weakness and powerlessness. But this was not God's intention. The word translated as submit is the Greek hupŏtassō[20], (pronounced hoop-ot-as'-so). Hupŏtassō could have been translated as obey, be under obedience, submit self unto.

An important note about hupŏtassō. It was a Greek military term meaning "to arrange [troop divisions] in a military fashion under the command of a leader".

In non-military use, it was "a voluntary attitude of giving in, cooperating, assuming responsibility, and carrying a burden".

Hmm, we'll come back to that in a moment.

---

[20] "G5293 - hypotassō - Strong's Greek Lexicon (KJV)." Blue Letter Bible. Web. 7 Jan, 2024. .

The word translated as resist is the Greek anthístēmi[21], (pronounced anth-is'-tay-mee). Anthístēmi means to stand against, oppose, resist, withstand, or set one's self against.

Submission is a voluntary action, and so is resistance.

No one forces us to submit. Not in the way God intended. He gave us free will because He wants us to choose.

Submitting to God is not about cowering because of His supernatural power. It's voluntarily giving up our plans and desires and choosing His.

It's making a daily choice to follow Christ. Even though there are tribulations and trials. It's choosing to imitate Christ, though the world mocks us for it.

Resisting the devil is also a choice. It means identifying the sins that easily beset us and creating a plan not to fall prey to those sins.

Resisting the devil is a choice to obey God rather than give in to the desires of the flesh.

Success in spiritual warfare is a two-part process:

1. Submit to God.
2. Resist the devil.

If we resist the devil, but don't submit to God, we lose. If we submit to God but don't resist the devil, we also lose.

Is any of this easy? No. Our sinful nature means that we want to sin. It means that we find it easier to sin.

But the Holy Spirit gives us the power to resist temptation. He reminds us of the truth of God's Word and empowers us to live

---

[21] "G436 - anthistēmi - Strong's Greek Lexicon (KJV)." Blue Letter Bible. Web. 7 Jan, 2024. .

by it.

You can do all things through Christ, my friend. Submit to God. Resist the devil and he will flee from you.

Prayer

Abba Father,

I submit to You. I give You all my desires, fears, needs... everything I am today and will be in the future.

I don't want to give into my fleshly desires anymore because that only leads to failure. I want You to take full control of my life, heart, and mind.

Give me the strength and power to resist the devil. In Jesus' name, Amen.

18

God Is Greater

Little children, you are from God and have overcome them, for he who is in you is greater than he who is in the world. 1 John 4:4

Since the inception of sin, humanity has lived with the specter of the enemy. We have built him up to be a formidable foe.

Please don't misunderstand. Don't underestimate or trifle with the enemy. The devil is powerful, dangerous, and bent on destroying you, but God is greater than he is.

We find the best illustration of these two opposing forces in 2 Kings 6:8-23.

Aram was at war with Israel, but whenever he planned an excursion, Elisha told the king of Israel and foil Aram's attempts.

The king of Aram couldn't understand how Elisha anticipated his every move and accused his men of being traitors.

When he found out the real threat to his dominance of Israel was Elisha, he was determined to mitigate the threat.

One morning, Elisha's servant got up and realized the city where they lived was surrounded by a mighty army. His first response was fear.

And no wonder. He and his master were two unarmed, untrained men against a superior army.

But Elisha wasn't afraid. He knew the army on his side was greater than that of the enemy.

After Elisha's prayer, his servant's eyes were opened and the young man could see the vast army encamped around Elisha.

This story teaches us three things about spiritual warfare.

1. **Prayer is powerful.** When Elisha prayed, there was an immediate response. Three times Elisha prayed in this brief account, and each time, God answered his prayer.

God's response to our prayers isn't always immediate, but He will answer.

2. **God is on our side.** If God had not been with Elisha, this story would have turned out differently. But Elisha served God with his whole heart and the Lord fought for him

3. **God's angels encamp around us, and they outnumber the enemy's.** The army of Aram surrounded Elisha at night while Elisha was asleep. But before the enemy could strike, the Army of the Lord was there.

We may not see the battles playing out in the spiritual realm, but rest assured, the angels of the Lord are fighting on our behalf.

My friend, the Spirit who lives in you is greater than the spirit who lives in the world. The word translated as greater in 1 John

4:4 is meízōn[22] (pronounced mide'-zone).

Meízōn is used in the Bible when referring to things that are bigger, greater, larger, older, stronger.

Meízōn means more *everything*! We don't have to fear the enemy because God is greater than he is.

Prayer

Dear Lord,

Open my eyes so I can see that the One who fights for me is greater than the enemy. Help me use the weapons You've given me to win this spiritual battle.

Prayer is powerful, Father. Please remind me to use it. Remind me You're on my side and You are greater than everyone who comes against me.

In Jesus' name, Amen.

---

[22] "G3187 - meizōn - Strong's Greek Lexicon (KJV)." Blue Letter Bible. Web. 7 Jan, 2024. .

19

God Fights For You

You shall not fear them, for it is the Lord your God who fights for you. Deuteronomy 3:22

Near the end of Moses's life, the great leader stood before the Israelites for one last speech. Moses recounted everything the Lord had done for them since their exodus from Egypt.

Moses reminded the people of all the kings they'd defeated on the way to the Promised Land to encourage them to keep going.

Because here's the thing: the Israelites were not warriors. They were a nation of slaves who served a mighty God.

It wasn't their military prowess or vast numbers that gave them victory in battle.

It wasn't their superior military strategies or guerrilla warfare tactics that netted them victory after victory.

The Israelites won battles because they followed the Lord of Hosts.

This was a key reminder as they moved toward inhabiting the space God had given them.

They didn't have to be afraid because the other nations had better weapons, bigger armies, or trained soldiers. They didn't have to be afraid because their enemies came to battle in chariots or on horses.

All they had to do was trust and obey.

Trust the God who had delivered them from Pharaoh.

Obey the Lord who has proven His faithfulness to Israel.

Trust the God who had given them victory over every nation on the east side of the Jordan to give them victory on the west side.

Obey the Lord who fought for them.

My friend, I'm not sure what battles you're facing today, but the advice remains the same.

The battle is not yours. It's the Lord's. Obey His commands and trust God to lead you to victory.

Prayer

Jehovah Sabaoth,

I am calling on You to give me victory over the evil one. The enemy has mounted an attack against me and I fear that I'll be overwhelmed.

Remind me, Lord, that I have no reason to be afraid because You are with me.

When I walk through the waters, it will not overcome me. When I walk through the fire, it will not burn me because You are with me.

I place this battle into Your hands because I trust You. Show me the path to take, Lord, and I will obey.

In Jesus' name, Amen.

20

God Is Your Guard

But the Lord is faithful. He will establish you and guard you against the evil one. 2 Thessalonians 3:3

As he wrapped up his second letter to the Thessalonians, the apostle Paul asked for prayers.

> *As for other matters, brothers and sisters, pray for us that the message of the Lord may spread rapidly and be honored, just as it was with you.*
> *And pray that we may be delivered from wicked and evil people, for not everyone has faith (2 Thessalonians 3:1-2 NIV).*

Then, as if something had triggered his memory, Paul wrote:

> *But the Lord is faithful. He will establish you and guard you against the evil one (2 Thessalonians 3:3).*

The word translated as faithful is the Greek pistós[23], (pronounced pis-tos'). Pistós is used in the Bible when referring to:

- People who show themselves faithful in the transaction of business, the execution of commands, or the discharge of official duties.
- Someone worthy of trust.
- Someone who can be relied on.

Don't these definitions perfectly encapsulate the nature of God's faithfulness?

The word translated as establish is the Greek stērízō[24], (pronounced stay-rid'-zo). Stērízō *literally* means to turn resolutely in a certain direction. It's also translated as make stable, place firmly, set fast, fix, strengthen, or confirm.

The word translated as guard is the Greek phylássō[25], (pronounced foo-las'-so). Phylássō could have been translated as watch, guard, preserve, or save. It's used in the Bible in the following contexts:

- to avoid, shun flee from
- to guard for one's self (i.e. for one's safety's sake) so as not to violate, i.e. to keep, observe (the precepts of the Mosaic law).

---

[23] "G4103 - pistos - Strong's Greek Lexicon (KJV)." Blue Letter Bible. Web. 7 Jan, 2024. .

[24] "G4741 - stērizō - Strong's Greek Lexicon (KJV)." Blue Letter Bible. Web. 7 Jan, 2024. .

[25] "G5442 - phylassō - Strong's Greek Lexicon (KJV)." Blue Letter Bible. Web. 7 Jan, 2024.

Okay, I know those were a lot of word definitions, so thanks for bearing with me. This is what I want us to focus on:

God is capable and can be trusted to shelter us from anything that will cause us harm. He can protect us from violating His Law.

That's why He sent us the Holy Spirit and gave us His Word. That's why we have Jesus as our example—a human being who lived a perfect life but didn't sin against God.

God is perfectly able to aid us in our quest to stand firm against the evil one.

God is your guard. Your protector. He's always on duty. He never gets sick and doesn't take days off.

God is always at work—protecting you against the evil one. You can trust Him to defend you.

Prayer

Jehovah Magen,

Thank You for being my shield, protector, and guard. Thank You for protecting me from the enemy and for providing the resources so that I can be faithful.

I am honored that You take such excellent care of me. You are trustworthy and faithful, God, and for that, I praise You. In Jesus' name, I pray, Amen.

21

Christ Has Overcome the World

I have said these things to you, that in me you may have peace. In the world you will have tribulation. But take heart; I have overcome the world. John 16:33

Tribulations, trials, hardship, struggle, strife, suffering, affliction, distress, pressure, stress...

I could keep going with all the words we use when describing the difficulties we face on Earth. These troubles seem to multiply when you're a believer. Some of them only exist *because* you're a disciple of Christ.

Many times, we struggle to understand why life is hard. Shouldn't it be easier because we follow Christ?

Didn't Jesus promise us an abundant life? Where's the peace and joy that's supposed to be ours when we became Christians?

If we studied the last exhortation Jesus gave to His disciples before His crucifixion, we'd find several dichotomies.

Jesus talked about faith and fear (John 16:1-2).

He spoke about grief and comfort (John 16:5-7). Mourning and joy (John 16:20-22). Trials and peace (John 16:33)

Some of those things make no sense in the same sentence until you remember who Jesus was talking to.

The disciples had many hard days ahead. But they also experienced wonder, awe, and joy.

They had their faith tested, but they also witnessed miracles. They *performed* miracles.

They were forsaken and abused. But they were also loved and cherished.

As Christ's followers, we share the fate of those early disciples. And like them, we have hope.

The word translated as peace is the Greek eirḗnē[26], (pronounced i-ray'-nay). Eirḗnē was used in the Bible when referring to:

- a state of national tranquillity
- exemption from the rage and havoc of war
- peace between individuals, i.e. harmony, concord
- security, safety, prosperity, felicity, (because peace and harmony make and keep things safe and prosperous)
- of the Messiah's peace and the way that leads to peace (salvation)
- of Christianity, the tranquil state of a soul assured of its salvation through Christ, and so fearing nothing from God and content with its earthly lot, of whatsoever sort that is
- the blessed state of devout and upright men after death.

---

[26] "G1515 - eirēnē - Strong's Greek Lexicon (KJV)." Blue Letter Bible. Web. 7 Jan, 2024. .

The word translated as overcome is the Greek nikáō[27] (pro-nounced nik-ah'-o).

Nikáō means to subdue, conquer, overcome, prevail, or get the victory.

We have peace because Jesus overcame the enemy. We have peace because Jesus defeated Satan.

Here's something mind-blowing. Jesus said this to the disciples *before* His crucifixion. He said this *before He died* and was resurrected.

Jesus could say that He had overcome the world *before the cross* because He knew who Jehovah was. Jesus knew that though the battle had raged long and hard, God was the victor.

Though the enemy has claimed this world as his own, his king-dom has an end. Unlike Christ, whose kingdom is everlasting (Daniel 2:44, 2 Peter 1:11).

Hallelujah! Christ has given us victory. We are overcomers because Jesus is. Trials will come. The enemy will attack. Spiritual warfare will continue until the end of the world.

But we don't have to worry because Jesus has overcome the world so that we can, too.

Prayer

Hallelujah Father,

I give You the highest praise because of who You are. You are the Creator of all things, the Eternal, Omniscient, Omnipotent

---

[27] "G3528 - nikaō - Strong's Greek Lexicon (KJV)." Blue Letter Bible. Web. 7 Jan, 2024. .

One.

You are greater than all the forces that come against me. Through You and in You, I have victory.

I praise You, Lord, for You are wonderful and worthy to be praised. In Jesus' magnificent name, Amen.

VI

Wearing Your Armor

Spiritual Warfare is something you're going to be engaged in every day for the rest of your life. This means you'll have to put on your armor daily. You will have to pick up and wield your weapons every day.

22

How to Engage in Spiritual Warfare

I wrote this article in 2019 and it was first published on *Caribbean Faith Women*[28] *on March 14, 2019. The truths and teaching remain applicable today and so I wanted to share them with you.*

How to Engage in Spiritual Warfare

I've been engaged in spiritual warfare. For the past few months, I've been finishing a self-published book. The closer I got to the deadline, the more challenges I faced. I always find it interesting how God uses blog posts and writing assignments to teach me.

My shipping company—which is usually reliable—started moving at a snail's pace. Even though I had ordered my proof copy with more than a month to spare, I received it only about

---

[28] How to Engage In Spiritual Warfare https://www.cbnfaithwomen.com/2019/03/14/how-to-engage-in-spiritual-warfare/ Published March 14, 2019

two weeks before the release date. My husband and I got sick in the same week I was planning to complete the final edits for my book.

Two days before the release date, while I was still busy formatting the manuscript, my son called me in a panic thirty minutes before a major exam was scheduled to begin. Without the government-issued timetable, he wouldn't be able to take his exam. We rushed to bring it to him only to find out hours later that it hadn't been needed.

As I analyzed the events of the past few weeks, I knew I had been involved in spiritual warfare.

What Is Spiritual Warfare?

In a nutshell, spiritual warfare is the conflict that exists between the devil and his agents and God and His supporters. In Revelation 12:7–9, we read:

> *And war broke out in heaven: Michael and his angels fought with the dragon; and the dragon and his angels fought,*
>
> *but they did not prevail, nor was a place found for them in heaven any longer.*
>
> *So the great dragon was cast out, that serpent of old, called the Devil and Satan, who deceives the whole world; he was cast to the earth, and his angels were cast out with him (NKJV).*

As physical beings, we sometimes forget that the war mentioned in Revelation is still happening today. We think that because we can't physically see the enemy the war must not exist. But spiritual warfare is more insidious than that: it affects the soul, the very spirit of man.

Spiritual Battle in the Mind

And that's why it's important to remember that there's a spiritual battle in the mind. "What? You're crazy! What do you mean there's a battle in my mind?"

Let's talk about it for a second: have you ever noticed how the enemy comes at you? He's rarely straightforward in his approach. He uses people to frustrate you. He puts lies in your mind. Every temptation that we've ever given into was first a thought.

Like the time a lying spirit spoke through Ahab's prophets. In 1 Kings 22:19-23, the prophet Micaiah tells Ahab and Jehosophat that God had revealed a conversation to him.

The Lord asked who would convince Ahab to go up to Gilead Ramoth so he would be killed. And the devil showed up. He volunteered to be a "lying spirit in the mouths of [Ahab's] prophets".

We know it was Satan because who else could it have been? God is truth and cannot tell a lie and that applies to the angels who support him as well.

Spiritual Warfare in the Bible

After Satan was kicked out of heaven, he set his sights on Eve. He used his words and the subtlety of language to convince Eve that something she believed wasn't true. Satan can mess with our minds by putting suggestions and temptations in our hearts.

He can't physically force us to do anything—because he can't push through the barrier of free will—but he can influence us to choose things he knows are bad for us. He wants to separate us from God (Isaiah 59:2).

You see, the Great Deception was a war of words:

> *"Has God indeed said...? (Genesis 3:1)"*

Those four words caused a ripple effect in Eve's mind. I imagine her trying to recall exactly what she had heard. "Did God really tell us not to eat from every tree in the garden?"

We don't have a full account of what happened after Eve was created, but there is no record of God telling Eve what she could and could not eat. We do, however, have a record of him telling Adam:

> *And the Lord God commanded the man, saying, "Of every tree of the garden you may freely eat;*
> *but of the tree of the knowledge of good and evil you shall not eat, for in the day that you eat of it you shall surely die." (Genesis 2:16-17)."*

Let's assume one of two things happened:

1. God repeated the exact statement to Eve.
2. Adam repeated God's statement to Eve.

In either case, there is a slight variation between what God said and what the devil said. "You shall not eat of every tree of the garden" has a slightly different connotation than "of every tree of the garden you may freely eat".

No wonder Eve was confused! Up to that point she had been used to dealing with persons who were straight-forward in their speech. She wasn't used to playing word games.

Sister, the enemy hasn't changed his strategy. He still comes at us with linguistic challenges. He tries to get us to doubt the truth that God has revealed to us. He still uses physical things to distract us from the war occurring in the spiritual realm.

Fighting Spiritual Battles

You may be wondering what's the best way to fight an enemy you can't see. First, let me give you some grace, "You're not crazy. There is an enemy, and you are in a war." The most concise advice I've found for fighting spiritual battles is found in Ephesians 6:10–18:

Finally, my brethren, be strong in the Lord and in the power of His might.

Put on the whole armor of God, that you may be able to stand against the wiles of the devil.

For we do not wrestle against flesh and blood, but against principalities, against powers, against the rulers of the darkness of this age, against spiritual hosts of wickedness in the heavenly places.

Therefore take up the whole armor of God, that you may be able to withstand in the evil day, and having done all, to stand.

Stand therefore, having girded your waist with truth, having put on the breastplate of righteousness,

and having shod your feet with the preparation of the gospel of peace;

above all, taking the shield of faith with which you will be able to quench all the fiery darts of the wicked one.

And take the helmet of salvation, and the sword of the Spirit, which is the word of God;

praying always with all prayer and supplication in the Spirit, being watchful to this end with all perseverance and supplication for all the saints— (NKJV)

Here Paul refers to six key pieces of weaponry that make up the armor of God: shoes, belt, breastplate, helmet, shield, and sword. Let's pretend we're getting dressed as we look at each piece individually.

The Gospel Shoes

As Western women, we don't go anywhere unless we're wearing our shoes. Some of us spend hours trying to find the perfect pair, especially if we have a special occasion. Many of us have experienced the pain—and embarrassment—of shoe failure. So, we understand that our feet have to be protected if they're to take us anywhere. Without a strong foundation on the gospel of Christ, we're going nowhere fast.

The Belt of Truth

For the Roman soldier of Paul's day, the belt held a lot of equipment like a sword, ropes, and pouches for food rations. The belt was also instrumental in keeping the rest of the armor in place. Truth and integrity ought to be important to us—it should be the basis of our character.

The Breastplate of Righteousness

The breastplate was attached to the soldier's belt by a series of leather thongs. It protects the chest—heart, lungs, and other vital organs. Tell me, sister, how are you protecting your heart today? Are you hidden behind the righteousness of Jesus?

Without the protection of Christ's righteousness, we cannot stand in the presence of God and we will be defeated before our enemy.

The Helmet of Salvation

Okay, girl, I know the last thing you want to put on your freshly done hair is a clunky helmet, so let's pretend this helmet is a very fashionable and highly functional hat. It's going to protect your head from a blow to the skull.

How are you protecting your mind? Do you monitor the things that you let into your head? Do you capture every wayward thought? Or do you, like me, sometimes allow Satan to take you down some dismal paths you should have stayed away from?

The Shield of Faith

The Roman shield was a long, rectangular knee-to-chin shield. It protected the soldier from the arrows and spears of the enemy. It was big enough to hide behind when the enemy let off a barrage of arrows.

Girlfriend, how's your faith? Is it large enough to shield you when the enemy is in a full-fledged attack? Or, is it too small to protect you from a mosquito?

The Sword of the Spirit

Maybe you think that you're not strong enough to wield a sword. Or, you believe a sword is an outdated weapon. So how about this? How versed are you on B-66 warfare? Did you even know that the Bible had 66 books? When was the last time you spent a few minutes—or hours—digging into the Word of God?

Girl, I'm not ragging on you. I'm trying to encourage you—and myself—to get into the Word of God. That's where our power is. That's where we'll find all the weapons we need to ward off the enemy when he comes. That's how we're going to know what to do.

This is a real war and Lucifer isn't playing with us. He has taken off the gloves and is attacking us with all the force of his light years of experience and knowledge. The only way we can win these spiritual battles is by putting on the whole armor of God.

To continue the analogy, if we don't put on the entire outfit that God gave us, we are not going to have the results we want—plus we going to look tacky.

My friend, the spiritual battle begins in the mind. I encourage you to grab your Bible and start putting on the armor of God. And in a little while, we'll be able to call ourselves Warrior Women.

* * *

Thank you for reading The Battle Is Not Yours! *If you enjoyed this devotional, please consider leaving a review online or sharing about it on social media. Even a few words are appreciated and may get this book into the hands of someone who'll appreciate it.*

About the Author

Aminata Coote's passionate love affair with books began with an upside-down copy of Silas Marner. She's on a mission to help women understand the truth of the Bible for themselves—one book at a time.

She writes to point to a God bigger than our failings and provide hope to others. Aminata lives in Montego Bay, Jamaica with her husband and son.

Aminata Coote is the author of several Bible studies and devotionals. These include, *Through God's Eyes: Marriage Lessons for Women* and *Unwavering: How to Stand Strong in Your Faith*.

She also writes inspirational romance novels. Her novels, including *His Perfect Wife* and *A Husband for Christmas*, are available for purchase from your favorite online retailers.

Connect with Aminata on her website, hebrews12endurance.com, or on Instagram or Facebook @aminatacoote.

Sign up for Aminata's newsletter at https://tinyurl.com/Face FearEbook and get a copy of the free e-book *Face Your Fears*.

Other Books by the Author

Inspirational Contemporary Romance

Orange Valley Series
His Perfect Wife
His Perfect Match
His Perfect Family
His Perfect Choice

Christmas with the Porters
A Husband for Christmas
A Family for Christmas

The Firefighters of Orange Valley
Falling For Her Fake Wedding Date

Sweet Haven
The Mother of His Child

Standalones
The Doctor's Christmas Miracle

Christian Living
Face Your Fear: Choose Faith Over Fear
Affirmations for Christian Women: Biblical Affirmations for

Spiritual and Emotional Self-Care
7 Lessons on Endurance from Hebrews 12:1-2
Through God's Eyes: Marriage Lessons for Women
Unwavering: How to Stand Strong in Your Faith

Learn more about my books at https://tinyurl.com/ACooteBooks

www.ingramcontent.com/pod-product-compliance
Lightning Source LLC
Chambersburg PA
CBHW020132180726

47992CB00021B/2607